What Others Are Saying About On Your Own

"I am a recent graduate of Christian Women's Job Corp. I was given a copy of your book, *On Your Own*. I'm writing to let you know how helpful it was. It gave good tips on how to look for a job. It's been a long time since I've had to look for a job. The part about jobs was most helpful. I'll keep this book on hand to refer back to if needed."

—Amazon review

"A must-read for both the young and those striking out on their own. The author gives some very tried and true advice as well as many new ideas on helping people through the journey of life. This is an excellent book to guide young people to success in their lives. It offers advice on resume building, obtaining a job, and being successful in a career—all the information a person needs to live independently. The book contains excellent chapters on time management and stress reduction techniques."

—Ken Culver, College Instructor

"Concise yet Comprehensive! Second semester seniors would definitely benefit from a course that utilizes this book as the text to help them transition life with more ease and expertise. When conducting corporate training I am continually shocked by the lack of basic consideration of co-workers and elemental grooming in the work place. Author Jumper touches on all these potential offenses. From now on the checks I give as graduation gifts will be tucked inside this helpful book that covers all that great instruction parents give that is not heard."

—Janna Beatty, parent, professional consultant

On Your Own

Workbook

Navigating the Road to Independence

JoAnn Jumper

On Your Own Workbook: Navigating the Road to Independence

Published by Wheatmark®
610 East Delano Street, Suite 104, Tucson, Arizona 85705 U.S.A.
www.wheatmark.com

ISBN: 978-1-60494-499-0
LCCN: 2010931731

Table of Contents

Introduction

The *Workbook-On Your Own: Navigating the Road to Independence* is designed to be a companion tool for use with the book of the same name, *On Your Own: Navigating the Road to Independence.* The book itself is intended to provide tips and techniques to anyone seeking independence. The book should be helpful not only for youth wanting to gain independence but also for those entering college, or individuals who have experienced abuse, neglect, unemployment, divorce, or homelessness.

The *Workbook* allows students the opportunity to practice many of the techniques they will read about in the book. By using these worksheets, students may become more proficient in dealing with many of the situations they are likely to encounter as they travel on their road to independence.

There is also a free guide for mentors, teachers, or facilitators who wish to use this workbook as part of a class or other group to assist group members with a more efficient transition to independence. The name of this publication is *Instructor's Manual- On Your Own: Navigating the Road to Independence.* This manual will serve to facilitate use of both the book and the companion workbook and may be downloaded at no cost from the website www.onyourown-instructorsmanual.blogspot.com.

The instructor's manual provides many helpful activities, including lists of materials necessary to implement those activities. These activities may be used to help the students become more skilled at applying the information found in *On Your Own: Navigating the Road to Independence.*

Workbooks may be ordered in bulk at www.wheatmark.com.

Chapter 1
Managing Finances

It is important to read Chapter 1, Managing Finances, in
On Your Own: Navigating the Road to Independence
to gain the greatest benefit from the following exercises.

Routine Expenses

Make a list of all of the expenses for which you are responsible. This list may reflect the items you are now responsible for or, if you choose, this may be a list of the items you feel you will be responsible for in the near future, once you have a job and are on your own.

Your list will probably include housing, utilities, gas, food, and medicine. Do not forget to include a category for entertainment and one for snacks. In order for this exercise to be helpful it is important to be sure you include all of your routine expenses. It is a good idea to include a category for miscellaneous expenses that you may not have each month, for instance birthday presents.

_____

_____

_____

_____

_____

_____

_____

_____

_____

_____

_____

_____

_____

_____

_____

_____

_____

_____

_____

_____

_____

_____

Budget Worksheet

On the chart below, list each item that you have decided is a regular expense. Determine how much you spend for each entry. Most people will set these expenses up as monthly expenses. It may be more appropriate for you to list these expenses as weekly expenses. Often people decide how to list these expenses based on whether they will be paid weekly or monthly.

Categories of Expenses	Anticipated Costs
Rent	
Electricity	
Water	

Annual Budget Worksheet

This chart allows one to keep track of the amount of money spent each month in each of the expense categories over a one year period. This can be a very helpful tool for budgeting for the next year, but can also be a quick reference if any of this information is needed when renting an apartment, applying for a loan, or completing income tax information.

Year _____

Expenses	Jan	Feb	March	April	May	June	July	Aug	Sept	Oct	Nov	Dec
Rent	350	350	350									

Sample Paycheck

Below you will find a sample paycheck. Each company's check might have a slightly different layout, but most checks contain the information shown below. The amount shown in the check is the net amount an employee might receive. (Please refer to Chapter 1, Managing Finances in *On Your Own: Navigating the Road to Independence* for a description of gross and net pay.)

The first set of numbers in the upper right corner of the sample check is the check number to use when recording the check information in a check ledger. The first set of numbers at the bottom left of the check is the bank's routing number. This is the bank's identification number and is used when corresponding and carrying out transactions with other banks. The second group of numbers on the bottom line is the checking account number from which the check is written and funds will be withdrawn. The last group of numbers is the number of this specific check (which is also in the upper right hand corner).

JJones, Inc. 123 N. 12 Street Any City, Texas 22222	Date: May 12, 2009	No. 222222222
Pay	Five hundred fifty dollars and 00/100	****550.00
To The **Order of**	Samantha S. xxxx Adams St No Where, TN. 55525	
	NON-NEGOTIABLE CHECK ADVICE	
1234567	7654321	222222222

Sample Paycheck Stub

Attached to paychecks you will usually find a paystub. The paystub gives all of the details about the number of hours worked, salary rate, vacation days, sick leave, and any deductions (including taxes) that have been taken from your gross pay. Below is a sample paycheck stub. Be sure you understand all of the deductions that are taken from your paycheck. If you are doing contract labor (meaning you are responsible for paying the taxes instead of your employer), you may not find any deductions on your paystub.

Below is a sample paystub. See if you can identify vacation time earned, amount of taxes deducted, and gross pay. Be sure you understand all of the figures on your paystub.

Employee Number: 123				Pay Rate: 7.50	Pay Period 5/18/1009

Hours Worked: 20	Tax Withheld 30.00	Insurance 5.00	Retirement 2.00	Misc. Deductions 0	

Current Pay:	Gross	Taxable Wages	Taxes	Deductions	Net	Unused Vac.	Unused Sick
	150.00	148	30	7.00	113.00	5	15
YTD	500.00	485	90	21	339.00		

Practice Paycheck

Fill out a sample paycheck.

Company Name		Date:		No.
Pay **To The** **Order of**				
1212121212	11111111	141414		Check No.

Practice Paystub

Using different pay rates, gross pay, deductions, etc., practice filling out a paystub to see the differences the various deductions make in your net pay.

Employee Number:					Pay Rate:		Pay Period
Hours Worked:		Tax Withheld	Insurance		Retirement	Misc. Deductions	
Current Pay:	Gross	Taxable Wages	Taxes	Deductions	Net	Unused Vac.	Unused Sick
	150.00	148	30	7.00	113.00	5	15
YTD	500.00	485	90	21	339.00		

Sample Check

Practice filling out a check that you would write to someone else for purchases or services. The line that follows the "$" sign is for you to enter the numbers representing the amount of the check ($100.00). The line below is for you to write in words the amount of the check (one hundred dollars). Be sure to fill in the "For" line so that you can remember exactly what this check was written for. The last line on the bottom right is for your signature.

Mr. or Mrs. John S. Smith   8888
9999 So. 12th Mission, MA 55555
255-222-3333

_____Date

Pay to the
Order of _____ $_____

_____ Dollars

Bank name and address

For _____   _____

XXXXXXXX   XXXXXXXXXXXX   8888

Practice Deposit Slip

Mr. or Mrs. John S. Smith
9999 So. 12th
Mission, MA 55555
255-222-3333

Date _____

_____
Signature for cash received

Bank name and address

XXXXXXXX   XXXXXXXXXXXX   8888

Cash _____

Checks _____

_____

_____

Subtotal _____

Less Cash_____

$ _____

Sample Check Ledger

It is critical to maintain a check ledger so that you have a record of all of the transactions in your checking account.

"Number" refers to the check number you are using. "Date" is the date you are writing the check. "Transaction" is to whom the check is being written, and "Payment" is the amount of the check. The "x" is to be used whenever you verify your transactions with the bank (usually with a monthly statement the bank will mail or email to you). When you make a deposit to your account you will enter it under "Deposit". The last column titled "Balance" will show the amount of money you have left in your account after writing a check or making a deposit.

Number	Date	Transaction	Payment	X	Deposit	Balance

Grab Box Contents

A Grab Box is a container that is preferably fire proof and can be easily "grabbed" in the event of a fire, tornado, or other catastrophe that requires you to quickly leave your residence. Copies of all important documents should be kept in this container. A list of everything in the Grab Box should be kept at a separate location in case you are unable to remove your Grab Box in an emergency.

Examples of some of the items that would be important to include in your Grab Box are Social Security Cards, insurance papers, bank account numbers, and passports.

Decide what you will use as your Grab Box. Below make a list of the items you are placing in your Grab Box.

_____
_____
_____
_____
_____
_____
_____
_____
_____
_____
_____
_____
_____
_____
_____
_____
_____
_____
_____
_____
_____
_____
_____
_____
_____

Chapter 2
Resume Writing

It is important to read Chapter 2, Resume Writing, in
On Your Own: Navigating the Road to Independence
to gain the greatest benefit from the following exercises.

Strengths and Weaknesses

No matter who you are, you have your own set of strengths and weaknesses. It is important to spend time thinking about your strengths and weaknesses because often times you will be asked about those traits by a potential employer. If you are uncertain about these characteristics, ask family members and friends how they would describe you to someone else.

What may often be viewed as a weakness can be modified to become a strength. For instance, someone who talks too much may learn to modify how much and when they are talking. Their ability to talk freely can then become a strength, as many people are very uncomfortable talking to others, particularly when they are talking to people they don't know well or when they are speaking in front of groups.

The "gift of gab" can be a real asset for people employed in jobs that require them to meet people easily, make presentations, or work with a large number of people.

Below list 8-10 strengths and 8-10 weaknesses that describe you. If you are having trouble thinking of some characteristics refer to the next page to see if some of those traits describe you.

Strengths   Weaknesses

_____   _____
_____   _____
_____   _____
_____   _____
_____   _____
_____   _____
_____   _____
_____   _____
_____   _____
_____   _____
_____   _____
_____   _____
_____   _____

Personality Characteristics

If you are uncertain of the characteristics that describe you, review the list below to see if some of these describe you.

Strengths	**Weaknesses**
outgoing	bossy
consistent	insecure
orderly	too sensitive
positive	manipulative
inspiring	worrier
loyal	headstrong
cheerful	domineering
respectful	anger easily
peaceful	stubborn
planner	resentful
patient	impatient
self-reliant	forgetful
funny	show-off
independent	uninvolved
leader	critical
adaptable	hard-to-please
considerate	loud

Skills List

As you begin to think about the various skills you have, you may feel that you don't really have very many. However, there are a number of behaviors that qualify as skills that can be helpful in the working world.

Perhaps you were in charge of a group of students to plan an activity or complete an assignment. As you think about that situation you may find that you displayed a great deal of leadership in bringing the assignment to completion. Leadership is a valued skill.

You may have worked at McDonald's and were expected to keep the customers happy. Relationship skills are extremely important in all workplaces. If you were in charge of employees you must have demonstrated some management skills.

Reflect on the various situations in which you have been and the roles you played. If you continue having trouble listing skills, ask your friends and family members about the skills they have observed in you. List below the types of skills you have demonstrated.

_____
_____
_____
_____
_____
_____
_____
_____
_____
_____
_____
_____
_____
_____
_____
_____
_____
_____
_____
_____
_____

Work Experience

Below list any previous work experience you have. Start with your current position, if you are now working. Then progress in reverse chronological order giving your most recent job, before your current one, then the one prior to that, etc.

Dates of Employment: _____ Organization/Position: _____

Job Responsibilities: _____

_____

_____

_____

_____

_____

Contact person: _____

Dates of Employment: _____ Organization/Position: _____

Job Responsibilities: _____

_____

_____

_____

_____

_____

Contact person: _____

Dates of Employment: _____ Organization/Position: _____

Job Responsibilities: _____

_____

_____

_____

_____

_____

Contact person: _____

Dates of Employment: _____ Organization/Position: _____

Job Responsibilities: _____

_____

_____

_____

_____

_____

Contact person: _____

Volunteer Experience

When writing your resume be sure to include any volunteer experience you have. Employers realize that individuals who volunteer are likely to be self-starters and are able to look beyond themselves and consider the needs of others. This means an individual may be a good team player.

Dates of Service: _____ Organization: _____
Total Hours Served: _____
Supervisor's Name: _____
Responsibilities: _____
_____
_____
_____
_____

Dates of Service: _____ Organization: _____
Total Hours Served: _____
Supervisor's Name: _____
Responsibilities: _____
_____
_____
_____
_____

Dates of Service: _____ Organization: _____
Total Hours Served: _____
Supervisor's Name: _____
Responsibilities: _____
_____
_____
_____
_____

Dates of Service: _____ Organization: _____
Total Hours Served: _____
Supervisor's Name: _____
Responsibilities: _____
_____
_____
_____
_____

Resume Writing

On the following four pages you will find sample resumes that represent a chronological resume, functional resume, and combination resume. Please look carefully at each of these resumes to note the differences in each.

Note that all resumes include dates of employment for every job held. If you do not work for a year or two because you had a baby, returned to school, or were seriously ill, you might want to include those dates and explain about the gap in time. If you were incarcerated you might want to put the dates representing the gap in employment on your resume and write something like "I will discuss this time frame during an interview". (This will give you an opportunity to convince the potential employer that you have changed your behavior and will be an excellent employee, in spite of a previous mistake.)

The following resumes do not have headings for

- Awards Received

- Specialized Training

- Languages Spoken

- Hobbies and Interests

- Extra Curricular Activities

If you have information that would appropriately fit under the above headings, certainly feel free to include that. Be sure that the information is relevant to the job for which you are applying. An employer wanting to hire someone to be a nurse may not care that someone likes to knit or work on cars.

Note that there is a significant amount of white space on the resumes and that the headings allow one to quickly find a category they might be interested in reading.

These resumes can be used as models for writing your own resume. This is a very important task as this may be the first way someone learns about you. Make it your best work. It will take some time to put a resume together, but it is worth it.

Refer to Chapter 2, Resume Writing, in *On Your Own: Navigating the Road to Independence* for further tips on writing a professional-looking resume.

(This resume is a Chronological Resume)

John R. Smith

1203 S. Indiana Street
Philadelphia, PA 55220

215-518-9045
johnr@xyz.com

Job Objective: Position as Physician's Assistance

Experience:

2007- present   Johnny's Urgent Care Clinic. Employed as Physician's Assistant to three physicians. Interview and diagnose patients, perform routine medical procedures, prescribe medications as needed.

2002-2007   University Medical Center. Worked as Physician's Assistant providing emergency diagnosis and treatment to patients reporting to the hospital emergency room.

2000-2002   Attended school (see below).

1998-2000   Dental Clinic of Philadelphia. Performed all office responsibilities including scheduling, insurance reimbursement, payroll, and management of office employees.

Education: Philadelphia University, Master Degree, Physician Assistant, 2002

University of Texas, Bachelor Degree, Psychology, 1998

Awards: University of Texas Gamma Phi Beta

References Furnished Upon Request

(This is a Functional Resume)

Susie Q. Jones

876 Northside
Richland, VA. 22222

245-777-0909

Objective: Restaurant Hostess

Qualifications: Hosting
Table Waiting
Sales
Leadership

Related Experience:

Hosting
--Hosted at local Red Lobster restaurant for two years.
--Interacted with customers and other employees.
--Managed seating arrangements with wait-staff schedules

Table Waiting
--Served tables at the Hilton Hotel for eighteen months.
--Interacted with customers, coworkers and supervisors.
--Demonstrate positive relationship skills with customers.

Sales
--Worked as sales associate at local ATT phone store for
   three years.
--Sold phones and contracts to individuals and businesses.
--Solved equipment problems
--Upgraded services and equipment.

Leadership
--Supervised other employees at all previous jobs.
--Revised and managed schedules.
--Led teams in implementing new procedures at all
   previous jobs.

Education and Training:

Graduated Richfield High School, 1999
Leadership Training, 2001

References Available Upon Request

(This is a Combination Resume)

Johnny Jingles

1125 Abby Lane
Cold Town, ND, 30003

Objective: Long Term Care Administrator

Qualifications: Ten years of experience in a variety of positions in long term care facilities including various positions.
Administrator
Activities director
Charge Nurse
Licensed Vocational Nurse

Experience:

Administration
--Currently administrator of 100 bed facility
--Responsible for 200 employees, 100 residents, facility management, developing and managing a budget of three million dollars.

Activity Director
--Developed and implemented at least two activities daily for residents, coordinated activities outside of the facilities, arranged programs involving community individuals to be conducted at the facility.

Charge Nurse

--Provided supervision to 5 nurses on the evening shift who were responsible for providing meds and medical care within the facility.

Licensed Vocational Nurse
--Provided day-to-day personal care of residents in long-term residential facility

Chronological Data:
2007-present -Administrator, Happy Hills Long Term Care Facility, Houston, Texas
2004-2007   -Activities Director, Happy Hills Long Term Care Facility, Houston, Texas
2002-2004   -Registered Nurse Nursing Supervisor, Sunny Days Nursing Facility
1998-2000   -Licensed Vocational Nurse, Sunny Days Nursing Facility

Education:
2007 -Long Term Care Administrator License, McLennan Community College
2004 -Activity Director's License, McLennan Community College
2002 -Masters Degree, Registered Nursing, University of Texas
2002 -Registered Nursing Bachelor Degree, University of Texas
1998 -Licensed Vocational Nurse, McLennan Community College

Resume Cover Sheet

Some people choose to put a cover sheet on their resume to give it a more finished look. Below is a sample of how a cover sheet might look. It should be very brief and serve to put your name easily before a potential employer.

Resume

John Smith
(Address)
(Contact number or email)

Personal Notebook

Over your work career you will be gathering a number of work-related documents. Organizing this information can save a great deal of time. An efficient way to do this can be to create a Personal Notebook. The purpose of the notebook is to keep all work related information organized and in one place that is easy to access. Whenever you need to write a new resume, document continuing education hours, or present a sample of your work, you will know exactly where to find the necessary information.

When you begin this process you may find that you have very few items to place in your notebook. Over time you will gather items and documents that you will want to add. Many of the items you may want in your notebook, for instance your diplomas, should be copies of the original document. You may have the original document framed or filed in a safe place.

Every individual's Personal Notebook will look very different. You may decide to use a loose leaf notebook with dividers that will allow you to easily add items to your notebook. Some people may find it easier to use a file cabinet and arrange their items in file folders. Whatever system you decide to use should be one that is efficient and makes sense to you.

Some individuals will include copies of verification of workshops they attended, samples of projects they have completed, and/or letters of recommendation they have received. Below are some suggestions to get you started. Determine what other categories you will want to include in your Personal Notebook.

Categories

Resume

Letters of Recommendation

Awards

_____

_____

_____

_____

_____

_____

_____

_____

_____

_____

Telephone Voice Messages

Voice messages can be unique and individualized. This is certainly your choice. Up until now all of the calls you have received may have been from friends who like to hear that "Hot Mama" is not available or they may like to listen to the latest popular songs in a loud volume. However you are now entering the professional world where people are watching and listening to how you handle yourself.

So while you are job searching, it is a good idea to be sure that the voice message your caller hears is very clearly spoken, understandable, and without background music. Some appropriate suggestions are listed below.

Message 1: You have reached the voice mailbox of _____. I am sorry I am unable to take your call at this moment. Please leave your name, number, and the time of your call and I will be happy to return your call as soon as possible at the earliest opportunity.

Message 2: This is _____. I am unavailable to take your call at this moment. Please leave your name and number and I will return your call a soon as possible.

Be sure to sound interested in having received their call. Also, include both your first and last name in your message. Do not use nick names like "Fat Jack" or any other names your friends may affectionately call you. Do not have the television or loud music playing in the background, or kids or family members yelling when you are recording your message.

Below write a few messages you feel might be appropriate. When you decide which message you like the best, record that on your phone. (You can always go back to your old messages once you are employed, unless you will be receiving business calls on your personal phone.)

_____

_____

_____

_____

_____

_____

_____

_____

_____

_____

Chapter 3
Searching for a Job

It is important to read Chapter 3, Searching for a Job, in
On Your Own: Navigating the Road to Independence
to gain the greatest benefit from the following exercises.

Job Searching Data

There are many approaches to searching for a job. For example searching the internet, looking in the newspaper, etc. List below the ways in which you intend to search for a job.

_____

_____

_____

_____

Organize the initial information you obtain in your search.

Agency/Location:_____

Contact Person:_____

Phone Number: _____

Job Title/Responsibilities: _____

_____

_____

Agency/Location:_____

Contact Person:_____

Phone Number: _____

Job Title/Responsibilities: _____

_____

_____

Agency/Location:_____

Contact Person:_____

Phone Number: _____

Job Title/Responsibilities: _____

_____

_____

Agency/Location:_____

Contact Person:_____

Phone Number: _____

Job Title/Responsibilities: _____

_____

_____

Job Contacts/References

Searching for a job is a full time job in itself. This is the time when it is appropriate to contact those people who are part of your support team, are influential contacts, and others who have offered to help in the past. Make a list of any individuals who fit into this category. This might include past bosses or supervisors, family friends, or people from your church.

Below make a list of the individuals you have identified and their contact information. In the second column, record the date of contact and in the third column, any relevant notes regarding your contact. If you need do a follow up contact you will have a record of when you spoke to someone and a note of when you are to contact her again.

Contact/Reference	Date	Notes

Possible Contacts/References

Title:_____Name:_____Connection:_____
Address:_____ __
_____Email:_____
Phone:(Work)_____(Cell)_____(Home)_____
Job Information: _____Letter of Recommendation:_____Other: _____
Comments:_____
_____
_____
_____

Title:_____Name:_____Connection:_____
Address:_____ __
_____Email:_____
Phone:(Work)_____(Cell)_____(Home)_____
Job Information: _____Letter of Recommendation:_____Other: _____
Comments:_____
_____
_____
_____

Title:_____Name:_____Connection:_____
Address:_____ __
_____Email:_____
Phone:(Work)_____(Cell)_____(Home)_____
Job Information: _____Letter of Recommendation:_____Other: _____
Comments:_____
_____
_____
_____

Title:_____Name:_____Connection:_____
Address:_____ __
_____Email:_____
Phone:(Work)_____(Cell)_____(Home)_____
Job Information: _____Letter of Recommendation:_____Other: _____
Comments:_____
_____
_____
_____

Sample Job Application

Position Applying For: _____

Personal Information

Full Name: _____

Address:_____

Contact Information: (home)_____ (cell) _____ (other) _____

Email: _____

Driver's License Number: _____ State: _____

Have you ever been disqualified from driving? No _____ Yes _____ If "yes", explain _____

_____

_____

Employment History

Current Employer-Name and Address (or last employer if currently unemployed) _____

_____

Job Title and Responsibilities: _____

Average Gross Pay: (hour, week, month): _____

Reason for Wanting to Leave Current Employment: _____

_____

_____

Below list previous employment giving the employer's name, address, job title/responsibilities, and dates of employment for the last 10 years. Explain any gaps in employment history.

Employer:_____

Address: _____

Job Title/Responsibilities: _____

_____

Dates of employment: _____

Employer:_____

Address: _____

Job Title/Responsibilities: _____

_____

Dates of employment: _____

Employer:_____

Address: _____

Job Title/Responsibilities: _____

_____

_____

Dates of employment: _____

Employer:_____

Address: _____

Job Title/Responsibilities: _____

_____

_____

Dates of employment: _____

Employer:_____

Address: _____

Job Title/Responsibilities: _____

_____

_____

Dates of employment: _____

Education

Please give the dates of attendance and the names of the schools you have attended beginning with high school. Indicate when you completed each school and the degree earned.

Dates	Institution	Completed	Degree

References

Two written references from people to whom you are not related are required. One of these references must be your current or most recent employer.

Name of Reference:_____

Position:_____

Company Name:_____

Company Address: _____

Name of Reference:_____

Position:_____

Company Name:_____

Company Address: _____

All positions are subject to a criminal background check and drug test.

Sample Interview Questions

Reviewing sample questions can help you prepare for an interview. By deciding on answers to these questions in advance, you will find you are more likely to be more confident and relaxed during an actual interview. This will help you keep from stumbling and pausing as you answer the interviewer's questions.

1. Tell me about yourself.

2. What are your greatest strengths and weaknesses?

3. What do you think you will be doing in 5, 10 years?

4. What qualifications do you have that make you suited for this job?

5. How do you define success?

6. How would you describe yourself? How would your friends describe you?

7. What motivates you to do your best?

8. What do you know about our company?

9. What is/was your favorite subject in school?

10. Why should I hire you?

11. What do you think will be your greatest personal challenge?

12. What frustrates you when working with others?

13. Do you have plans to further your education?

14. What is your greatest accomplishment?

15. In what kind of work environment are you most comfortable?

16. How do you feel your past experiences will help you in this position?

17. Describe how you would handle a work situation in which a coworker is trying to get you to do her work?

18. Explain how you would handle an angry customer?

19. Which of your personal skills do you think will benefit you the most at our company?

20. Do you have any questions for me? (They will expect you to have some questions.)

Practice Interview Feedback Sheet

This sheet is to be completed by those people conducting practice interviews.

Date: _____

Interviewee: _____

Strengths noted in interview: _____

_____

_____

_____

Suggestions for future interviews: _____

_____

_____

_____

Date: _____

Interviewee: _____

Strengths noted in interview: _____

_____

_____

Suggestions for future interviews: _____

_____

_____

_____

Date: _____

Interviewee: _____

Strengths noted in interview: _____

_____

_____

Suggestions for future interviews: _____

_____

_____

_____

Interview Summary Sheet

As you complete an interview, it will be helpful to fill out the information listed below. A few days after completing an interview, you may find it difficult to remember the answers to the following questions. It is best to complete this form as soon as you complete your interview.

Date of Interview:_____

Agency/Organization:_____

Name of Interviewer:_____

Summary of Interview Content:_____ __

_____

_____

Additional Information/Questions:_____

_____

_____

_____

_____

Follow up Date:_____

Date of Interview:_____

Agency/Organization:_____

Name of Interviewer:_____

Summary of Interview Content:_____ __

_____

_____

Additional Information/Questions:_____

_____

_____

_____

_____

Follow up Date:_____

Sample Thank You Note

Writing a thank you note to someone who took the time to interview you is always a good thing. This note should be typed on stationary or hand written inside a thank you card. Email is not an appropriate way to express your appreciation for a job interview. Below is a suggested format for writing a professional thank you note.

Mr. John Mathis
123 Main Street
Memphis, TN 33333

September 14, 2009

Dear Mr. Mathis,

Thank you so much for taking the time to interview me on September 13, 2009. I enjoyed my time with you and learned a great deal of information about your organization. It was very interesting to learn how your company has grown.

I think I am very well suited for the position of _____ for which I interviewed. I look forward to hearing from you soon regarding the position.

Again, thank you for visiting with me.

Sincerely,

John Smith

134 East Terrace

Austin, TX 66666

Sample Envelope

Note on the envelope that the complete name and address of the sender is in the upper left corner of the envelope and the title (Mr., Dr., etc) of the recipient is used in the mailing address.

John Smith
134 East Terrace
Austin, TX 66666

STAMP

Mr. John Mathis

XYZ Organization

123 Main Street

Memphis, TN 33333

Chapter 4
Keeping Your Job

It is important to read Chapter 4, Keeping Your Job, in
On Your Own: Navigating the Road to Independence
to gain the greatest benefit from the following exercises.

Employee Questions for Employer

Now that you are hired, you may have some questions you did not previously ask of the potential employer. Below are a few questions to get you started. Add to the list any additional questions you would like to ask of the employer prior to starting your job.

1. What is the dress code?

2. Is there a particular spot for employees to park?

3. Do you provide orientation training prior to actually beginning work?

4. Are employees expected to take their lunch break on the premises?

5. Are cell phones allowed at work?

List any additional questions that you might wish to ask.

_____
_____
_____
_____
_____
_____
_____
_____
_____
_____
_____
_____
_____
_____
_____
_____
_____
_____
_____
_____
_____
_____
_____

Workforce Behaviors

Your behavior on the job may make the difference in whether or not you keep your job. There are a number of behaviors that can bother coworkers and supervisors and result in difficulties on the job. Below are listed some of the problem behaviors. List all of the behaviors you can think of that will help you be successful on the job. Refer to Chapter 4 in *On Your Own: Navigating the Road to Independence* for other suggestions.

Problem Behaviors:

Eating someone else's food from the refrigerator

Leaving trash around

Smoking in a non-smoking area

Poor hygiene

Trying to get others to do your work

List below the positive behaviors that should help you be a good coworker and employee:

_____
_____
_____
_____
_____
_____
_____
_____
_____
_____
_____
_____
_____
_____
_____
_____
_____
_____
_____

Workplace Frustrations

Any job you hold will likely have frustrations associated with it. It is helpful to be aware of those work related situations that create frustration for you and to develop ways to handle those frustrations before they become major problems.

Below are some examples that might cause frustration on the job. List other things that you might find frustrating.

Frustrations might develop when coworkers or supervisors:

1. use their cell phones to talk or text when they are supposed to be working.

2. pass their work onto others.

3. do not return phone calls or emails promptly.

4. use your personal computer when they should be using their own.

5. touch and move things around on your desk.

6. do not return things they borrow.

List any additional frustrations for you and discuss with a peer or supervisor how you might handle these situations.

_____

_____

_____

_____

_____

_____

_____

_____

_____

_____

_____

_____

_____

_____

_____

_____

_____

_____

Communication Styles—"I"- Messages

Communicating effectively can be critical in maintaining healthy relationships whether the relationship is with coworkers, supervisors, friends or family members. The three basic types of communication are passive, aggressive, and assertive. There may be situations where any of these forms of communication can be effective, however, being able to communicate assertively is generally the best way. Communicating assertively allows individuals to express how they feel about a particular situation without hurting others or allowing others to take advantage of them.

Descriptions of three basic types of communication are:

passive- not expressing your feelings or emotions, but simply agreeing with someone else. Your feelings are "stuffed" and you generally say what you think others want to hear.

aggressive- is more of an "attack", i.e., "you are so stupid", "why do you feel that way", "what an idiot". Often loud voices and yelling accompany aggressive communication.

assertive- allows you to share your opinions and feelings without the other person verbally attacking or denying how you feel.

A very important skill to learn is how to communicate using "I"-messages. "I"-messages contain three parts, *how* one feels, *why* they feel that way, and *when* they feel that way. If you communicate to someone and include all three parts you are much more likely to feel that you have been heard and are more likely to maintain healthy communication with the individual with whom you are speaking.

Let's pretend you are waiting on a coworker to complete his/her part of a project so that you may complete your part. The deadline is close and the coworker is talking to a friend on the phone instead of working on the project.

If you communicate with the coworker by saying, "Gosh it is getting late.", you have communicated *passively* and will probably be ignored by the coworker. You have not made your feelings known.

If you were to say in a loud voice, "Can't you get off the phone. Don't you see what time it is?", you have communicated *aggressively*. With this communication style the coworker will probably get mad and may slow down completing her part even more.

To clearly express yourself *assertively*, you might say, "I am really feeling *anxious* (feelings) because *I am unable to complete my part of this project* (why) *until I have your part and you are talking on the phone to your friend and not completing your part of the project* (when).

When using "I"-messages, you must use an actual feeling word. If you were to say, "I feel *like decking* you", you are describing a behavior, not a feeling. "I"-messages are great to use when expressing positive feelings as well. "I am so *proud* (feeling) of you *for making all "A"s and "B"s* (when) *because I know how hard you studied* (why).

"I"-messages can be used in virtually any situation. You may find that if people are resistant, you may need to give several "I"-messages. If you continue to express your opinion giving each of the three parts, there is nothing that the receiver of your message can do to deny how you are feeling.

Assertive communication is an excellent way to communicate with your parents, spouse, siblings and children as well.

The more you practice this approach, the more skilled you will become. You likely will find that relationships you care about become more positive.

Practice using "I"-messages with some of the situations you have been in with a friend or teacher.

_____

_____

_____

_____

_____

_____

_____

_____

_____

_____

_____

_____

_____

_____

_____

_____

_____

Communication Parts

Any communication that takes place has four parts to it. The parts are the sender, message, channel, and receiver. The sender is the person who is trying to tell someone something. The message is the actual content or words. The channel is the way in which the message is communicated and the receiver is the person to whom the message is going.

Difficulty can occur in any one of these parts of communication. If there are times when you feel you have not been understood, look at each of the parts of the message you sent and try to determine which part of your communication might be creating a problem.

Below list as many possible problems that might occur in each part of a communication attempt.

Sender-

_____
_____
_____
_____

Message-

_____
_____
_____
_____

Channel-

_____
_____
_____
_____

Receiver-

_____
_____
_____
_____

Think about a recent conversation in which you feel you did not clearly communicate your message. Review in your mind where the breakdown might have occurred. Practice how the message might have been more clearly communicated. (You cannot always make changes in the receiver for instance, if they are hard of hearing, angry or not willing to listen.)

"Oreo" Method of Communication

There may be a time in which you need to confront someone with uncomfortable information. You certainly don't want to hurt their feelings, however, you may have some criticism to give. One way of doing this is by using the "Oreo" method. When using this method you sandwich the criticism in between two positive comments. Perhaps you have a coworker who is reporting to work late and that impacts your ability to do your job effectively.

Using the "Oreo" method you might say, "I really like the way you handle your part of our project. Your coming in late, however, makes it difficult for me to complete my work. Since you play an important part in this project, I look forward to you arriving on time so we can complete this assignment.

Try using the "Oreo" method with someone you know who will not clear up his or her area, thereby making it a problem for you. Or, think about another personal situation in which you might apply the "Oreo" method. It may take some practice, but it will become natural with time.

Situation:

_____

_____

_____

_____

_____

"Oreo" Statement:

_____

_____

_____

_____

_____

_____

_____

Taking Responsibility

In any area of your life it is very important to learn to take responsibility for your own behaviors, good or bad. Employers appreciate those employees who are willing to take responsibility for their behaviors and mistakes. Everyone makes mistakes at one time or another. When this occurs it is critical that an individual assumes responsibility for their behavior.

In most cases you will find that employers will work with someone who admits to a mistake and apologizes for having made that mistake. If an employer finds that an employee did not accept responsibility for his or her behavior, the employee will likely be fired. When someone does not take responsibility for his or her behaviors, this will often result in others not being able to trust that person.

Taking responsibility can be very uncomfortable, particularly if you did something wrong, or didn't do something you should have that results in problems for other employees or your company. You can diminish this discomfort by saying from the very beginning, "I am responsible for this. I am very sorry that I _____. What can I do to correct this situation?" Or, "How can I help make up for this mistake?"

Employers want employees on whom they can depend. Failing to apologize may make the employer feel that you really don't care what happens to your job or the organization.

If there is a problem that resulted from someone else's negligence, it might be appropriate to say, "I am not the person responsible for this situation, but I would like to help correct it." Employers love to have someone offer to help and to be a team player.

Think about a situation in which you would need to apologize. (You can make one up.) Below write the apology and make an offer to correct the situation.

Situation:

_____

_____

_____

_____

Apology:

_____

_____

_____

_____

_____

Pros/Cons Sheet

Throughout life you will be faced with many situations that force you to make difficult decisions. A Pro/Cons Sheet is a tool that can help you make these decisions more easily.

At the top of a sheet, write a situation that you are trying to resolve. An example might be "Should I go to a community college vs. a four year institution?" Review the sheet below and see how one student resolved this dilemma.

Pros	Cons
1. no housing expenses as can stay at home (this might be a negative!)	1. housing expenses
2. could keep current job	2. would need to find another job
3. tuition is much lower	3. tuition much higher
4. can get adjusted to college before leaving home	4. would need student loans
5. can hang with current friends	5. will miss getting to meet new friends
6. no student loans	
7. can take more credit hours at school because of lower cost	
8. mom will do laundry	

As you can see in this example it becomes clear that attending a community college at this time is the best decision for this student. For each student posed with this question, the pros and cons comments will be different, however, one decision or the other will generally present itself as the better option.

A benefit to using the Pros/Cons Sheet is that whatever the decision, by working through this process the decision is made based on facts instead of emotions.

Reflect on a decision you are struggling with. Complete a Pros/Cons Sheet and see if the right decision becomes clearer.

Pros	Cons

Problem Solving Approach

Some situations that need resolution require more effort that using the Pros/Cons Sheet. The following approach requires several steps but can be very helpful in identifying steps that may need to be taken to solve a problem.

This particular problem solving approach has several parts to it. They are as follows:

Step 1. State the problem clearly.

Step 2. Generate possible solutions.

Step 3. Determine possible consequences to each of the possible solutions.

Step 4. Select a solution.

Step 5. Implement the solution.

Step 6. Evaluate the solution.

At any point in this approach you may realize that what you thought was the original problem is actually not, that it is something else. This is part of the value of this approach. If you do not clearly define the problem, anything you do to solve it will not be effective. If you decide you do not have the problem correctly defined, return to Step 1, restate the problem and then work through the other steps again.

To demonstrate this approach, let's assume that you have a roommate who will not clean up after herself.

Step 1. The problem is that Jenny will not clean up after herself, leaving the apartment a wreck.

Step 2. Possible solutions-

       a. clean up the apartment myself

       b. hire someone to do this

       c. talk to Jenny about this

       d. throw all of her things away

       e. get another roommate

(Be sure to write down *any* possible solution even if it is totally unrealistic.)

Step 3. Determine possible consequences to each of the above possible solutions, and cross out the consequences you do not like.

      a. ~~I will be doing all of the work and Jenny will not do her part.~~

      b. ~~I cannot afford to pay someone to do this.~~

      c. She would understand my feelings if I communicate this correctly and would probably be willing to clean up her items.

      d. ~~Jenny would probably get mad, and expect me to pay for her items. This would ruin a great friendship~~

      e. ~~I don't know of anyone else to room with and I like Jenny a lot~~

Step 4. After you strike through the consequences you do not like, the best consequence becomes clear.

Step 5. Now you can decide when you will talk to Jenny, how you will word your feelings, and what each of you can do (clean up every Saturday, everyday, etc) to solve the problem. You may decide together that each evening you will ask Jenny to clean up and she agrees to do it at that time.

Step 6. Set a time when you will evaluate your plan. Will you decide in one week, one month, etc., if this approach is working or not? If it is not, you will need to decide if you are really working on the correct problem, or if the problem is something else. You need to generate other possible solutions.

Following the process above, choose a problem you are currently dealing with at work or at home and apply the above steps. Being able to manage an approach like this often makes you feel less emotional about the situation and more in control of what the outcome will be.

Chapter 5
Finding Your Own Place to Live

It is important to read Chapter 5, Finding Your Own Place to Live, in
On Your Own: Navigating the Road to Independence
to gain the greatest benefit from the following exercises.

Rental Property Qualifications

Below are some qualifications you might want to have in the property you are going to call home.

Check the qualifications you hope to find in a property you rent. The first two items require a number to be placed in the blank.

_____ Number of bedrooms

_____ Number of bathrooms

_____ Central heat and air (as opposed to window units and space heaters)

_____ Utilities are paid by the landlord

_____ Appliances are provided and maintained by the landlord.

_____ Washer and dryer provided

_____ Washer and dryer connections (you would provide your own washer and dryer)

_____ Off-street parking

_____ Fenced yard

_____ Furnished (landlord would provide couch, tables, etc.) Be sure to clarify exactly what is included if the apartment is furnished.

_____ Additional storage space

_____ Garage? If so, is it attached to the primary residence?

_____ Yard maintenance?

_____ Pets? What kind?

Additional questions to ask of landlord: _____

_____

_____

_____

_____

_____

Rental Application
XXXXXX Rentals

(Please Print)   DATE: _____

NAME: _____

CURRENT ADDRESS: _____

CURRENT LANDLORD:_____ LANDLORD'S PHONE: _____

YEARS AT CURRENT ADDRESS: _____CURRENT RENT PAYING:_____

EMPLOYER: _____ PHONE: _____

EMPLOYER'S ADDRESS: _____

POSITION: _____ LENGTH OF EMPLOYMENT: _____

SPOUSE'S NAME: _____

SPOUSE'S EMPLOYER: _____

EMPLOYER'S ADDRESS: _____

POSITION: _____ LENGTH OF EMPLOYMENT: _____

NUMBER TO OCCUPY: _____ ADULTS: _____ CHILDREN: _____

BANK: _____

CREDIT REFERENCES: (list three please)

NAME	ADDRESS	PHONE

DRIVER'S LICENSE NO: _____ STATE: _____ VEHICLE LICENSE NO: _____

Subject to approval of the application a _____ security deposit and the first month's rent of _____is due.

Utility Company Information

It is important to know the cost of deposits and connection fees for each of the utilities for which you will be responsible. The landlord may be willing to give you an approximate or average monthly cost of the utilities for the residence you are considering leasing. If you lease this residence, this information should help in planning your budget. This will also help you decide if you can afford cable and internet connections.

Name of utility company: _____

Amount of deposit: _____

Set up and other additional charges: _____
_____
_____

Name of utility company: _____

Amount of deposit: _____

Set up and other additional charges: _____
_____
_____

Name of utility company: _____

Amount of deposit: _____

Set up and other additional charges: _____
_____
_____

Name of utility company: _____

Amount of deposit: _____

Set up and other additional charges: _____
_____
_____

Chapter 6
Setting Up Your Own Place

It is important to read Chapter 6, Setting up Your Own Place to Live, in
On Your Own: Navigating the Road to Independence
to gain the greatest benefit from the following exercises.

Furnishings

This list may be used to check off items you want in your residence as you gather them.

Kitchen

_____ Stove/hot plate/griddle/microwave

_____ Pots/pans

_____ Refrigerator

_____ Glasses

_____ Plates

_____ Silverware

_____ Table and chairs

_____ Mixer

_____ Cooking utensils

Living Room

_____ Couch/chairs

_____ Window coverings

_____ Lamps

_____ Tables

Bedroom

_____ Bed

_____ Linens-sheets and pillows, pillow cases

_____ Comforter

_____ Lamps

_____ Bookcase

_____ Night stand

Bathroom

_____ Shower curtain

_____ Towels

_____ Soap

_____ Toilet tissue

_____ Personal hygiene items

Miscellaneous

_____ Cleaning supplies

_____ Mop, broom

_____ Laundry detergent

_____ Clock

_____ Smoke alarm

_____ Carbon monoxide detector

Valuables

As you look around your residence you may realize that there are some items that would be expensive or difficult to replace. By making a list of these items and their replacement value, you may decide that it is smart to obtain insurance on the contents in your home.

Item	Replacement Value

Chapter 7
Handling Personal Responsibilities

It is important to read Chapter 7, Handling Personal Responsibilities, in
On Your Own: Navigating the Road to Independence
to gain the greatest benefit from the following exercises.

Regular Expenses

Below list all of the regular expenses that you currently have. You may want to include a category for gifts and one for miscellaneous expenses. As you list these expenses arrange them by the frequency that they are due, for instance, weekly, monthly, or yearly.

Creditor	Amount

Yearly

_____

_____

_____

_____

_____

_____

Monthly

_____

_____

_____

_____

_____

_____

_____

_____

_____

_____

_____

Weekly

_____

_____

_____

_____

_____

This chart should help you keep track of your regular expenses and decide which bills need to be paid from each paycheck, depending on whether you are paid daily, weekly, or monthly.

Self Care Checklist

Regular medical checkups are important to help prevent health issues in the future. This checklist will help you keep track of routine checkups.

Type	Frequency	Last visit
Medical		
Dental		
Eye Exam		

Insurance Information:

Name of Insurance Company: _____

Name of Insured: _____

Group Number: _____

Effective Date: _____

Pharmacy Information:

Name: _____

Location: _____

Phone Number: _____

Personal "Cheerleaders"

Generally, people who are on the road to independence have had some, if not many people, who have helped them along the way. These "cheerleaders" may have helped through teaching skills, lending support, listening to problems, loaning money, or through other efforts. It can be helpful as you gain independence to reflect on these individuals who were helpful to you and how they helped. You may sometime want to return the favor and be of help to someone else. Everyone needs a helping hand at some time in their lives.

See how many people you can recall who have made a difference in your life.

Individual	How They Helped	Result of the Help

Social Service Agencies

Serving others in need can help payback some of the individuals who may have helped you. It is also a great way to spend time and give to others who may not be as fortunate as you. Even though there are times when you feel things are really going wrong, there is always someone who is in greater need than you. Identify as many social service agencies in your community as you can and note the types of clients they serve (youth, aging, homeless, victims of domestic violence, etc.)

Social Service Agencies   Types of Clients Served

Individual Social Service Agency Information

Agency Name: _____

Agency Location: _____

Contact Person: _____

Population Served: _____

Volunteer Responsibilities: _____
_____
_____
_____
_____

Agency Name: _____

Agency Location: _____

Contact Person: _____

Population Served: _____

Volunteer Responsibilities: _____
_____
_____
_____
_____

Agency Name: _____

Agency Location: _____

Contact Person: _____

Population Served: _____

Volunteer Responsibilities: _____
_____
_____
_____
_____

Chapter 8
Managing Your Time

It is important to read Chapter 8, Managing Your Time, in
On Your Own: Navigating the Road to Independence
to gain the greatest benefit from the following exercises.

"Group and Contain"

People tend to be much more efficient with their time if their personal areas are organized. This would include your room, residence, locker, and/or office. The "group and contain" concept can be very helpful in organizing your environment.

Look around your personal space and see what messages it sends. For most of people there are some areas of clutter. If you are going to "group and contain" you might start by putting all like items together. This approach can be used with any items you want to organize. If you have swimming items like a beach towel, sun screen, sunglasses, lip gloss, etc., those can all be placed in a plastic bucket, box, or bag. When you are ready to go swimming you have everything together.

Once you have items grouped and contained, label them so that they are easy to identify on a shelf or in a cabinet.

Begin by organizing one area of your life. Make a list of the various categories you want to group and contain. For instance, find anything that would be considered office or school supplies. Put all rubber bands, paper clips, staplers and like items together. Now locate any kind of container, perhaps a butter tub, or small bowl and place all of the rubber bands in one, the paper clips in another, etc. Label each of the containers. Keep a trash can and a box marked "donations" close by for those items you no longer want.

Identify the various "groups" of items that you want to contain.

_____

_____

_____

_____

_____

_____

_____

_____

_____

_____

_____

_____

_____

_____

Calendar

A calendar can become your "best friend". Use a calendar to record appointments, the dates assignments are due, birthdays, and any other important information you want to remember. There are many styles available. Choose one you like and use it regularly.

Monday	Tuesday	Wednesday	Thursday	Friday	Saturday

TIME MANAGEMENT SCHEDULE

By recording regularly scheduled activities you will be able to quickly determine a good time to schedule medical appointments, car repairs, and visits with friends.

TIME	Monday	Tuesday	Wednesday	Thursday	Friday	Saturday	Sunday
6:30-7:00 AM							
7:00 7:30							
7:30-8:00							
8:00-8:30							
8:30-9:00							
9:00-9:30							
9:30-10:00							
10:00-10:30							
10:30-11:00							
11:00-11:30							
11:30 -12:00							
12:00-12:30 PM							
12:30-1:00							
1:00-1:30							
1:30-2:00							
2:00-2:30							
2:30-3:00							
3:00-3:30							
3:30-4:00							
4:00-4:30							
4:30-5:00							
5:00-5:30							
5:30-6:00							
6:00-6:30							
6:30-7:00							
7:00-7:30							
7:30-8:00							
8:00-8:30							
8:30-9:00							
9:00-9:30							
9:30-10:00							
10:00-10:30							
10:30-11:00							

Priority List

Keeping a list of tasks that need to be done will help you stay organized. This may be done by arranging things that need to be done each day, or by the location where you will be doing things, i.e., home, office, grocery store. Some people will divide a notebook sized paper into categories such as things to be done, calls to make, and bills to pay. As you get used to making a priority list each day or week, you will find the style that works best for you. Try the approach below and see how effective it is for you.

To-do's for the week of: _____

Errands to Run: _____

_____

_____

_____

_____

_____

Calls to make: _____

_____

_____

_____

_____

Bills to pay:_____

_____

_____

_____

_____

Daily Checklist

When you are in a hurry to get to work or school it can be difficult to remember everything that must be done before you leave the house. Make a list of those things that must be done in order to have your day go smoothly. You can review this list each day before leaving the house to ensure everything has been completed. Be sure to include packing your lunch, getting your purse or backpack, etc.

Things to do each morning:

_____

_____

_____

_____

_____

_____

_____

_____

_____

_____

Many people find it helpful to do many morning chores the night before so that they are not as rushed in the morning. This might include packing a lunch, laying out clothes, putting backpack in car, etc.

_____

_____

_____

_____

_____

_____

_____

_____

_____

_____

_____

Chapter 9
Managing Stress

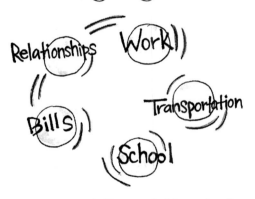

It is important to read Chapter 9, Managing Stress, in
On Your Own: Navigating the Road to Independence
to gain the greatest benefit from the following exercises.

Causes of Stress

Everyone experiences stress at various times in their lives. Stress can be positive (eustress) or negative (distress). Negative stress is what can cause problems for you. Sometimes the stress is minor and is merely an irritation. At other times stress can be severe, even to the point of keeping you from completing daily tasks. It can also affect your relationships with others. At any level, stress can wear on you. If stress continues over a long period of time it can affect your immune system resulting in serious illnesses.

One of the first things to do to manage stress is to determine what causes stress for you. Different things cause stress for different people. Something that causes stress for someone is called a stressor. By identifying the causes, you may be able to deal with stress earlier, therefore keeping the stress from harming you.

Make a list of those things that cause stress for you. Try to be specific. If school is one thing that causes stress determine if it is tests at school, projects done in a group, or a specific class that causes your stress.

1. _____

2. _____

3. _____

4. _____

5. _____

6. _____

7. _____

8. _____

9. _____

10. _____

Signs of Stress

Being aware of your individual signs of stress is the first step in learning to manage stress. You may already be aware of the obvious signs of stress like yelling at someone, or throwing things, but it is also important to learn the more subtle signs of stress as these are often the first indicators of stress. For some people, subtle signs are neck aches, sweaty palms, or tension headaches. There can be a wide variety of other signs.

People who are experiencing the same situations will often experience very different signs and degrees of stress. Two people may each have a flat tire. One may yell or scream while the other person paces and rubs his hands together because he is late for work.

Note your personal signs of stress. Don't worry if you are not aware of these signs. Many people are not aware of their stress signs until they begin paying attention to their bodies when they are in stressful situations.

_____

_____

_____

_____

_____

_____

_____

_____

_____

_____

_____

_____

_____

_____

_____

_____

_____

_____

_____

_____

_____

_____

Observation of Signs of Stress

Find a public location in which you can comfortably observe others. This might be a shopping mall, a park, etc. Record the various signs of stress that others are demonstrating. Some people "stuff" their feelings and stress so that others may not notice. It may become a problem for people who "stuff" their stress, because eventually these people will let all of these emotions out at one time, usually in a very inappropriate way. Hopefully, you will learn to manage your stress in a healthy way. You will learn some ways to do this in one of your later assignments.

Signs of Stress in Other:

_____

_____

_____

_____

_____

_____

_____

_____

_____

_____

_____

_____

_____

_____

_____

_____

_____

_____

_____

_____

_____

_____

_____

_____

_____

Positive Messages

When people are under stress or not feeling good about themselves they often have "tapes" with negative messages that continue to run through their heads. The message might sound like, "I am never going to pass that test", "I am so stupid", "Nobody likes me", etc. When people continue to repeat things like "I will never pass that test", they often don't pass. This is called a "self-fulfilling prophecy". Had the student changed the tape in her head to "I am going to figure out a way to pass this test", or "I am going to get a tutor so I can pass this test", there is a good chance they might have passed the exam.

You are the only one in charge of the messages that go through your head. Below list some messages that you find you say that are negative. Next to the negative message, change that negative message into a positive one. Practice repeating the positive message.

Negative Messages	Positive Messages

Stress Reducing Diet

Refer to page 102 in *On Your Own: Navigating the Road to Independence* for some of the foods that are helpful in reducing stress. List those foods that you might want to include in your diet to help reduce stress. Below plan a meal or two that include some of the stress reducing foods.

Meal One

_____
_____
_____
_____
_____
_____
_____
_____

Meal Two

_____
_____
_____
_____
_____
_____
_____

Meal Three

_____
_____
_____
_____
_____
_____
_____

Exercise Sheet

Exercise is one of the very best stress reducers. Even if one exercises for only a few minutes a day it can help reduce their level of stress. Often people will say, "I just don't have any time to exercise". That seems to be when they need exercise the most.

Record the date and length of time you exercise for one week. In the chart below, list various ways in which you might be able to increase the amount of exercise you do. Be sure to consider the time of day you find best to exercise and the type of activity you like doing.

Date	Length of Time

Ways to Increase Exercise

Chapter 10
Ensuring Safety and Security

It is important to read Chapter 10, Ensuring Safety and Security, in
On Your Own: Navigating the Road to Independence
to gain the greatest benefit from the following exercises.

Home Safety Checklist

There are many simple things that can be done to improve your likelihood of being safe. Below you will find a checklist of things that can be done at your home and away from home to be more secure. Review the suggestions on pages 104-7 of *On Your Own: Navigating the Road to Independence*. List below the things you would like to do to make your residence more secure and to protect yourself.

Changes to Make at Home

_____
_____
_____
_____
_____
_____
_____
_____
_____
_____
_____
_____
_____
_____
_____
_____

Behaviors to Implement Away from Home

_____
_____
_____
_____
_____
_____
_____
_____
_____
_____
_____
_____

Precautions Others Use

Either talk with other family members or friends, or observe other people in a public place. List below the types of precautions they use to ensure their safety while away from home.

_____

_____

_____

_____

_____

_____

_____

_____

_____

_____

_____

_____

_____

_____

_____

_____

_____

_____

_____

_____

_____

_____

_____

_____

_____

_____

_____

Travel Checklist

Check off the various precautions listed below before beginning a trip. With these preparations, you are more likely to avoid complications and be better prepared should something unexpected occur.

Vehicle

_____ check oil and fluids

_____ check tires/tire pressure

_____ practice changing a tire

_____ check to see that spare tire is in good condition

_____ check fuel level

Contacts

_____ Department of Public Safety (you might want to program this into your cell phone)

_____ emergency road service

_____ family member or friends

_____ family doctor

_____ insurance agent's number and documentation of insurance

Travel Items

_____ cell phone charger

_____ umbrella

_____ tool kit

_____ blanket

_____ snacks

_____ hotel reservation confirmation

_____ map

_____ first aid kit

_____ water

Emergency Contact List

Complete the list below. Make a copy of it to keep with you and one to store in another safe location.

_____ family member

_____ Department of Public Safety

_____ emergency police number (besides "911")

_____ fire department

_____ poison control center

_____ doctor's office

_____ pharmacy

_____ other

_____

_____

_____

Chapter 11
Succeeding in School

It is important to read Chapter 11, Succeeding in School, in
On Your Own: Navigating the Road to Independence
to gain the greatest benefit from the following exercises.

Classroom Information

Name of Teacher: _____ Class: _____

Contact Information: _____

When to Contact: _____

How grade is determined: _____
_____
_____

Attendance Policy: _____
_____
_____

Contact Information for Other Students:_____
_____
_____

Name of Teacher: _____ Class: _____

Contact Information: _____

When to Contact: _____

How grade is determined: _____
_____
_____

Attendance Policy: _____
_____
_____

Contact Information for Other Students:_____
_____
_____

Attendance Challenges/Solutions

Many students enrolled in school find that attending classes regularly can be one of the biggest challenges to being successful. Below list some of the things that make it difficult for you to attend classes. These might be things like not having gas money, over sleeping, or babysitters cancelling at the last moment.

In the second section list things you might do to try to minimize these challenges.

Challenges

_____
_____
_____
_____
_____
_____
_____
_____
_____
_____
_____
_____

Possible Solutions

_____
_____
_____
_____
_____
_____
_____
_____
_____
_____
_____

Classroom Behaviors

Refer to pages 116-20 in *On Your Own: Navigating the Road to Independence* to review the suggestions for appropriate behavior in the classroom. Below list some of the behaviors you might work on to improve your success in school.

_____

_____

_____

_____

_____

_____

_____

_____

_____

_____

_____

_____

_____

_____

_____

_____

_____

_____

_____

_____

_____

_____

_____

_____

_____

_____

_____

_____

_____

_____

_____

_____

_____

Study Habits

Identify those study habits that create problems for you in your classes. Next to them list things you might do to change or improve these behaviors.

Problem Behaviors	Behavioral Changes

Preparation for Tests

List below the ways in which you prepared to take your last test. In section two include additional things you might do in order to be even better prepared for your upcoming tests.

Usual Test Preparation Steps:

_____

_____

_____

_____

_____

_____

_____

_____

_____

_____

Additional Steps to Prepare for Tests:

_____

_____

_____

_____

_____

_____

_____

_____

_____

_____

_____

_____

_____

Goal Setting

Below is a model for setting goals. Select a behavior you would like to change. Be sure as you are setting your goal that it follows these guidelines:

The goal should:

      S- be specific

      M- be measurable

      A- have action steps

      R- be realistic

      T- include a time frame

      E- be evaluated

The steps in goal setting are to:

      1. state the goal clearly

      2. determine action steps

      3. implement the steps

      4. determine when and how to evaluate if the goal has been reached

      5. post the goal where you see it each day to help you complete this goal successfully

Also, your goal setting should:

      1. be objective

      2. be worded positively

      3. be attainable

      4. list specific steps to be taken to reach goal

      5. be measurable

      6. be future oriented

Review the goal below and see if it meets all of the criteria. If it does the goal-setter is likely to be successful. If any of these steps are missing, the goal will probably not be reached.

An example of a goal to be reached is

    1.Clearly define the goal

        I will lose 10 pounds in 3 weeks (there is a specific number of pounds and a specific time frame), the goal is objective (either the person did or did not lose 10 pounds), and it is measurable (getting on the scales)

    2. Action Steps

        a. exercise daily (must be specific, so add "for 30 minutes". How will you exercise? what time of day?)

        b. eliminate sweets (all sweets? only desserts?)

        c. eliminate soft drinks

    3. Implement the action steps

    4. I will weigh every Friday to determine if I am approaching my goal

    5. In three weeks, weigh and record. Has the goal been met?

If the goal has not been met, go back to the beginning and see if the goal was attainable or if the action steps need to be changed to reach your goal.

Select a goal that you are wanting to attain. Complete the steps on the following page and implement your goal!

Personal Goal Setting Sheet

Goal:

Action Steps:

Implement Action Steps: (date)

Evaluate Goal:

    When:

    How:

Changes to be made if you did not reach your goal:

_____

_____

_____

_____

_____

_____

_____

_____

_____

_____

_____

_____

_____

_____

Author's Note

I hope you have found these exercises and activities beneficial. There may be many times when you want to revisit the information in this workbook, depending on what is occurring in your life.

I wish you great success as you travel on your road to independence!

LaVergne, TN USA
23 November 2010

206049LV00004B/2/P